VICTORIAN
CONUNDRUMS

VICTORIAN CONUNDRUMS

A 19th Century Puzzler

Ken Russell
and Philip Carter

Michael O'Mara Books Limited

First published in Great Britain in 1998 by
Michael O'Mara Books Limited
9 Lion Yard
Tremadoc Road
London SW4 7NQ

A CIP catalogue record for this book is available from the
British Library

ISBN 1-85479-294-6

1 3 5 7 9 10 8 6 4 2

Designed by Mick Keates
Typeset by Concise Artisans

Printed and bound in Finland by WSOY

Whilst considerable care has been taken in compiling this book,
the publishers cannot accept responsibility for any errors
which may occur.

RANK AND FILE

The sergeant had fewer than 500 men to line up on parade. He tried arranging them in rows of three but found there was one left over. Then he tried them in rows of four, then five and six, but always there was one left over. Finally he tried them in rows of seven and, to his relief, saw that the rows were exactly even.

How many soldiers were lined up on parade?

SOLITAIRE

The marble in space number 1 has been removed. You must clear the board of every marble except one, and must finish in space number 1.

The marbles are removed by passing over an adjacent marble. Marbles can move vertically or horizontally in either direction, but not diagonally. No marble can be moved unless it jumps over and removes another marble.

The puzzle can be solved in just 31 moves.

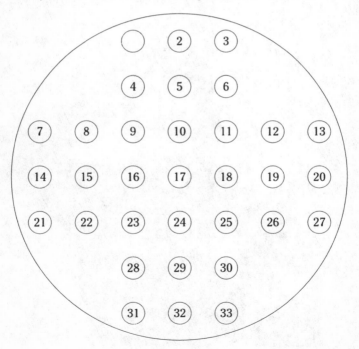

DOUBLET 1

Make BLUE PINK in 8 links.

BLUE

– – – –

– – – –

– – – –

– – – –

– – – –

– – – –

– – – –

– – – –

PINK

WORD PLAY

Rearrange all the letters in each of the sentences to form, in each case, a well-known proverb.

1. I don't admit women are faint.
2. It rocks. The broad flag of the free.
3. Strong lion's share almost gone.

NINE IN A ROW

A rich man had a dishonest butler who helped himself to bottles of wine, so the rich man set a trap. He had in his cellar twenty-eight bottles which he arranged in a square so that there were nine bottles on each side. The butler, realising the trap that had been set, helped himself to four bottles and rearranged the remainder so that there were still nine bottles on each side. Later he took a further four bottles and again rearranged the remaining bottles with nine on each side.

How did the butler rearrange the bottles on the two occasions?

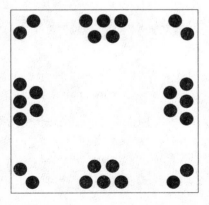

RELATIVELY SPEAKING

Gazing up at the portrait hung over the fireplace in his drawing room his lordship remarked:

'Brothers and sisters have I none,
but that man's father is my father's son.'

Who is in the portrait?

FORTY-FIVE

Find four numbers, the sum of which is 45, so that if 2 is added to the first number, 2 is subtracted from the second number, the third number is multiplied by 2 and the fourth number is divided by 2, then the four numbers so produced are all the same.

CASK OF WINE

While clearing out some vats in a wine factory some workmen came across a full eight-gallon cask that had not been sold. Because they were such good workers the owner said they could have the wine providing they could share it out equally using just two containers which he had available, one of which could hold five gallons and the other three.

The workmen successfully completed the task and earned the wine by pouring it from one container to another and not spilling a drop until two containers each held four gallons.

How did they perform the task? Neither the cask nor the two containers were calibrated in any way.

CUPS AND SAUCERS

Cook came across two cups and a saucer in the kitchen. Bored for something to do she weighed each item. Altogether they came to 12 ounces but the larger cup with the saucer weighed exactly double the smaller cup, while the smaller cup with the saucer weighed exactly the same as the larger cup.

What did each weigh?

DIVISION SUM

Fill in the missing figures to complete the long division sum.

```
_ 1 _ ) 8 6 _ 2 _ ( _ 7 _
        6 _ 0
        _ _ 6 _
        2 _ _ 5
         _ 5 7 _
          1 _ _ _
          _ _ _ _
```

BOYS AND GIRLS

By moving from square to square in a clockwise direction it is possible to spell out the names of six girls and five boys. You may only go to adjacent squares and move horizontally and vertically but not diagonally. It does not matter which name you identify first, if you take the correct route you will eventually spell out all eleven names and arrive back at your point of starting.

FE	LI	CI	ED	WI	N
EY	BR	TY	RY	DE	A
LY	AU	HE	N	RM	OT
L	CL	CE	IE	AT	K
PO	AR	I	HU	GO	MA
CE	EN	AL	NE	LI	DE

FOUR INTEGERS

ABCD represents four integers such that the following arrangements are square numbers.

What integer does each letter represent?

C A B A

D C B A

D A C B

CATCHING A THIEF

The constable had no problem catching the thief who was exactly 27 steps in front of him when he gave chase. While the thief took eight steps to the policeman's five, the policeman had a longer stride; in fact two of the policeman's strides were equal to five of that of the thief.

How many steps did the constable need to catch the thief?

FILLING A BATH

You have accidentally left out the plug and are attempting to fill the bath with both taps full on. The hot tap takes 6 minutes to fill the bath. The cold tap takes 2 minutes and the water empties through the plug hole in 4 minutes.

In how many minutes will the bath be filled?

BEHEADMENT RIDDLE

In yon vast field of cultivated space,
I there am found with members of my race;
Decapitate me – if you've no objection –
You then will find what brings me to perfection;
Take one more cut, and then you'll plainly see
What I am destined, day by day, to be.

COUNTERS

By moving just two counters at a time the object is in six moves to have all the black counters side by side and all the white counters side by side. Two counters must always be moved at a time and they must be adjoining counters. For example, for the first move you could move counters 5 and 6 into spaces 13 and 14, but you could not move counters 5 and 7.

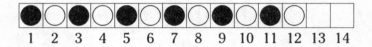

1 2 3 4 5 6 7 8 9 10 11 12 13 14

FOWL CALCULATIONS

A man buys a pheasant, two ducks and three hens for £4 0s 0d. The price of two ducks and three hens is the same as three pheasants; and three hens cost as much as two ducks.

What was the cost of each?
(In old money, £1 = 20 shillings)

VICTORIAN ANAGRAMS

I CRY THAT I SIN   (one word)

STOP AN INGRESS   (two words: 2, 11)

BOLD HEARTS FOUGHT
IN KENT   (five words: 7, 2, 3, 5, 5)

FLIT ON CHEERING ANGEL (two words: 8, 11)

THE
LINOLEUM PUZZLE

By H.E. Dudeney

Cut the piece of linoleum into four pieces that will fit together to form a perfect square. You may only cut along the lines.

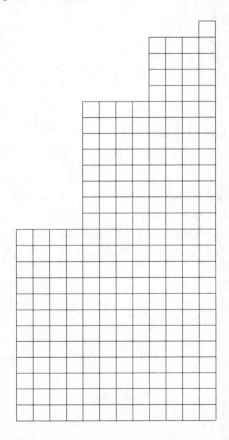

GRANDMOTHER'S BIRTHDAY

'How old is your son?' asked a man to his neighbour. 'My son is five times as old as my daughter and my wife is five times as old as my son. I am twice as old as my wife whereas grandmother, who is celebrating her eighty-first birthday is as old as all of us put together.'

How old is the man's son?

LITTLE TOMMY TITTLETAT

Little Tommy Tittletat took two Ts,
To tie two tups to two tall trees,
To torment the terrible tittletat,
How many Ts in all of that?

QUIET VERONICA

All anagrams of famous Victorians:

I COVER ANTIQUE

CABLE PRINTER

DISMAL INANER JIBE

HELL! DARN! ALGEBRA EXAM

THE CENTRAL ROBOT

SCREW HANDRAIL

INVITING ODD SLAVE

AMERICA HALF DAY

NERVY IRISH GRIN

ABHORRED SEWER GANG

PHALANX

Fill the circles with the number 1, 2, 3, 4 etc. up to 18 without having any unfilled circles left over. To start, choose a circle and put the number 1 in it. Then move left, right, up or down to a new circle and put a 2 in it. Diagonal moves are not allowed. You may not pass over unfilled circles but you may pass over circles already filled with a number. You may not retrace any part of your last move, so if you have just moved north-south your next move cannot be south-north.

There are several possible solutions, but you might find that discovering just one is deceptively difficult.

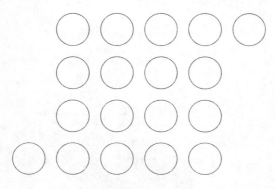

EIGHT EIGHTS

Write down eight eights so that they add up to one thousand.

AGES TEASER

Edward is twice as old as Benjamin used to be when Edward was as old as Benjamin is now.

Benjamin is 36. How old is Edward?

MAGIC PRIME

Using prime numbers only, each one once only, complete the square so that each horizontal, vertical and corner-to-corner line totals 219.

A prime number is one which is only divisible by itself and 1.

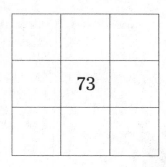

RING THE BELL

The fairground had come to town and there was great excitement because the owners were awarding prizes for the game of 'swing the hammer'. Anyone who was strong enough to ring the bell received a prize of £10, anyone who scored 95 received 10 shillings and anyone scoring 90 received 2/6d.

Altogether over the weekend the owners paid out £100.

What was the breakdown of people who rang the bell, those who scored 95 and those who scored 90?

(In old money 10 shillings = 50 pence; 2/6d (half a crown) = 12.5 pence)

TOMATOES

The vicar returns from his allotment with a small bag of tomatoes. To the first parishioner he meets he gives half the tomatoes plus half a tomato, to the second he gives half what he has left plus half a tomato and to the third he gives half what he has left plus half a tomato. He has then distributed all his bag of tomatoes.

How many tomatoes did he initially have in the bag?

REBUS CONUNDRUM

The answer to this rebus is a classic conundrum.

What is the conundrum, and what is the answer to it?

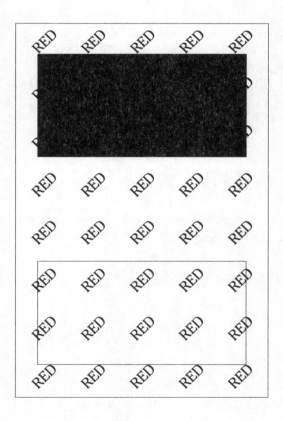

MIXED FRACTION

The only way to represent the number '18' in a mixed fraction using the digits 1–9 once each only, is to cheat slightly in the following way:

$$18 = 9 + \left(\dfrac{5742}{\frac{638}{1}} \right)$$

Can you find a similar way to represent the number '15'?

THREE ANIMALS

Use all letters of this sentence once each only to spell out three animals.

'TALL ELEPHANT OR APEMAN'

THE TWO YOUNG ENTREPRENEURS

Two children were selling bags of sweets on street corners. Each started the day with 300 bags of sweets. Matthew sold his sweets at two bags for one penny and Amy sold hers at three bags for one penny.

On the second day they again had 300 bags each but decided to go into partnership and sell the sweets at five bags for two pennies. Thus, they would each get a penny from each sale of five bags.

Who benefited on the second day?

PALINDROMES

Complete the palindromes (sentences which read the same backwards and forwards) with the help of the letters already inserted.

1. _ _ M _ _ _ _ _ _ _ _ _ _

2. _ O _ _ E _ _ _ _ _ G _ _?

3. _ _ _ _ M _ _ _ , _ _ _ _ _ O _

4. _ _ _ _ _ _ , I _ _ _ _ _ , _ ' _ _ D _ _

5. _ N _ _ , _ _ O _ _ _ _ R _ _ _ _ _ _ _ _ E
   _ _ M _ _ _ _ I _ _ _ _

6. D _ _ , _ O _ _ ; _ _ _ S _ _ _ T, _ F _ _ _
   _ E _ _ _ _ _ _ _ _ N _ _ _ _ _ _ _ _ _ _ , _
   D _ _ _ _ _ _ _ _

THE MAGIC HEXAGON

Insert the remaining numbers 1 to 12 into the circles so that each of the six lines of four numbers adds up to 26.

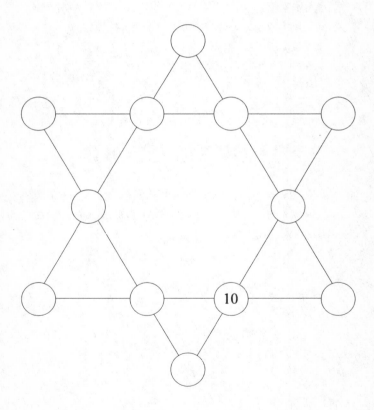

THE URBAN RIDDLE

By John Edward Field

Come near, O men of wisdom, and search you
    through my ditty:
Four buried in this rubbish cities fair are
    lying low,
Search 'til on every line you see stand up
    a risen city.
'Til walls and arches, terraces and turrets,
    upward grow.

STRIKING CLOCK

It takes the town hall clock 6 seconds to strike
4 o'clock in the afternoon. How long does it take
to strike midnight?

THREE CLASSICS

1. A famous anagram by Lewis Carroll:

   Do you know a one word anagram
   for 'new door'?

2. Queen Victoria loved anagrams but this one, for
   some reason, had her stumped:

   ABONETY

3. This one, for some reason, seems to bamboozle
   most people:

   ROASTMULES

DOUBLET II

By Lewis Carroll

Put loaf into oven in 9 links.

L O A F

- - - -

- - - -

- - - -

- - - -

- - - -

- - - -

- - - -

- - - -

- - - -

O V E N

TALL TREE STORY

A boy is 3.5 feet tall and records his height by hammering a nail in a tree and carving his initials, date and height by the side of it. Five years later he returns to the same tree and finds that it has grown by, on average, 14 inches per year.

How high now, is the nail from the ground?

BACKWARDS AND FORWARDS

A man is walking his dog on the lead towards home at a steady 4 mph. When they are nine miles from home the man lets the dog off the lead. The dog immediately runs off towards home at 9 mph. When the dog reaches the house it turns round and runs back to the man at the same speed. When it reaches the man it turns back for the house. This is repeated until the man gets home and lets in the dog.

How many miles does the dog cover from being let off the lead to being let into the house?

CHILDREN'S CAKES

Each is an anagram of a Charles Dickens book title:

CHARM SOCIAL STAR

LIVID RED FACED POP

DIRTY SCHOOLHOUSE TIP

STEW VITRIOL

EXASPERATING OCTET

NOISY CHICKEN BALL

SIMPLE ADDITION

If eleven plus two equals one, what does nine plus five equal?

STRANGE
SUBTRACTION

How can you take two from 5 and leave 4?

OLD PALS

Albert meets Ernest whom he hasn't seen or heard of since they were school chums 40 years ago.

Albert asks Ernest how many children he has and he replies 'Two'. 'Is the older one a girl?' asks Albert. 'Yes', replied Ernest.

What is the probability that both children are girls and what would the probability have been if Albert's second question had been 'Is at least one of them a girl?' ?

MAGIC WORD SQUARE

This puzzle first appeared in 1859. The answers are all 6-letter words and when entered in the grid will read the same both across and down.

1	2	3	4	5	6
2					
3					
4					
5					
6					

1. Surround
2. Legendary Greek killed when the sun melted his wings
3. Most uncommon
4. Bring into being
5. Gloss, sheen
6. Think highly of

THE EIFFEL TOWER

When completed in 1889 the Eiffel Tower was something of a sensation. Designed by the French engineer Alexandre-Gustave Eiffel its height is 492 feet plus half its own height.

How high is the Eiffel Tower?

GRANDPA'S PARTY

My grandfather and his twin brother held a joint birthday last week and invited their entire family. They both have an equal number of sons who, in turn, have as many sons as they have brothers, all surviving. The combined number of all these sons and grandsons is equal to the age of my grandfather, who in three years time will be exactly three times my own age.

How old is my grandfather, how old am I and how many grandsons received invitations to the party?

PENNIES

Why are 1888 pennies worth more than 1887 pennies?

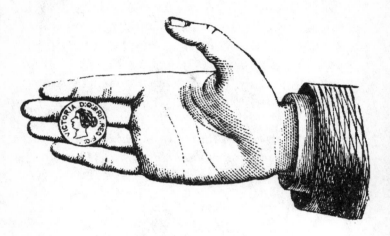

TWO FRACTIONS

1, 2, 3, 4, 5, 6, 7, 8, 9, 0

Use the digits above once each only to compose two fractions which when added together equal 1.

TEN TREES

'I don't mind how you plant these ten saplings,' said the head gardener to his assistant, 'as long as they are in a symmetrical pattern, and there are five rows of four trees each.'

'How do I do that?' asked the assistant.

'There are several ways,' replied the head gardener, 'but you must figure them out for yourself.'

In how many different ways was it possible for the gardener's assistant to carry out the task which he had been set?

WAS IT A CAT I SAW

By Sam Lloyd

In how many ways can the palindrome 'was it a cat I saw' be read by starting with 'w' and then moving up and down, left or right (but not diagonally) to adjacent letters until you reach the central letter 'c', and then back to the border again? In each attempt you may not visit the same lettered square more than once.

					W					
				W	A	W				
			W	A	S	A	W			
		W	A	S	I	S	A	W		
	W	A	S	I	T	I	S	A	W	
W	A	S	I	T	A	T	I	S	A	W
W	A	S	I	T	A	C	A	T	I	S	A	W

W	A	S	I	T	A	T	I	S	A	W
	W	A	S	I	T	I	S	A	W	
		W	A	S	I	S	A	W		
			W	A	S	A	W			
				W	A	W				
					W					

THE FIVE PENNIES

Someone tosses five coins in the air at the same time and you are betting on the outcome. What are the chances that at least four of the coins will finish up either all heads or all tails?

TREASURE TRAIL

The treasure is on the square marked 'T'. To reach it you have to find the starting square which will take you through every one of the 63 remaining squares once each only before arriving at the treasure.

'1S' means one square south, 4W means four squares west.

3S 3E	1E 1S	1E 4S	2W 1S	3W 6S	1E 2S	4S 2W	1S 1W
2E 6S	1N 1W	2S 5E	5S 3E	1N 2E	4S 2W	2W 1N	4W 1N
1N 3E	1S 3E	3E 2N	1N 2E	1E 3S	1N 1W	1E 1N	5S 3W
2S 1E	6E 3S	1W 3N	1N 2E	3N 2W	1N 3W	2S 1E	4S 2W
1N 2E	1S 1E	2N 2W	1W 2S	4W 3N	1S 1W	T	1N 2W
1E 2N	6E 2S	2S 1W	2S 3W	3N 3E	1S 1W	1N 6W	2S 4W
1N 6E	2N 1E	4E 1S	1E 4N	2N 3E	6N 2E	2N 1W	2N 1W
1N 5E	2E 1N	1N 2W	4N 3W	3N 3W	4N 1E	5N 3W	2N 7W

COUNTERS

Pick up two adjacent counters at a time and in just four moves (two counters per move) finish with the counters in the position below.

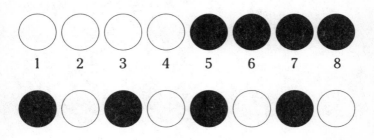

DOUBLET III

Prove that the rogue is a beast in 11 moves.

ROGUE

- - - - -

- - - - -

- - - - -

- - - - -

- - - - -

- - - - -

- - - - -

- - - - -

- - - - -

- - - - -

BEAST

PIECE OF CHEESE

Take a circular piece of cheese and divide it up by making six cuts of a knife. What is the greatest number of pieces that can be thus made?

The example shows seventeen pieces with six cuts.

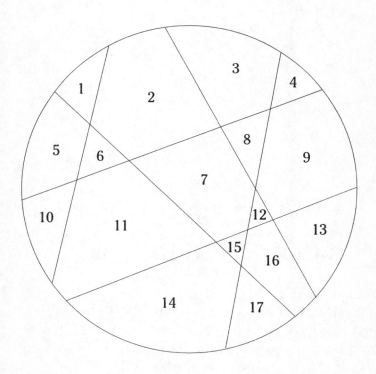

SQUARES

BY LEWIS CARROLL

Can the three squares be drawn without taking the pen off the paper, intersecting any line or going over any part of a line twice?

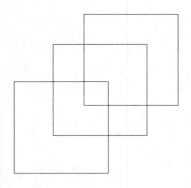

COUNTERFEIT COIN

In a pile of twelve coins, there is a single counterfeit coin which can be detected only by its weight. Using a balance scale, how can you find out in only three operations which coin is counterfeit and whether it is heavy or light?

DOUBLE ACROSTIC

Each couplet provides the clue to a word. Solve the clues and list the five words. Two more words will be spelt out by the first and last letters of the five words.

Tract of land green with grass,
Happy place for lad and lass.

I can prove it wasn't me,
Was making hay with Emily Lee.

Motive or logical point of view,
Here's the rhyme now it's up to you.

Jostling along with the pack,
Several elbows in my back.

Worry, torment, toil and trouble,
Lots of hassle at the double.

THE BY-ELECTION

In a recent by-election a total of 7396 votes were polled. The Liberal was elected by a majority of 592 over the Socialist, by 794 over the Conservative and by 962 over the Independent.

How many votes were polled for each candidate?

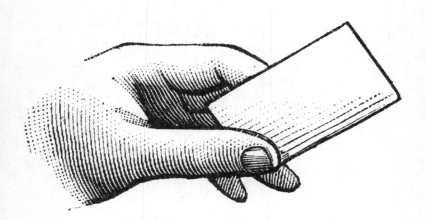

BAG OF POTATOES

'How much is this bag of potatoes?' asked the man.

'32lb divided by half its own weight,' said the greengrocer.

How much did the bag of potatoes weigh?

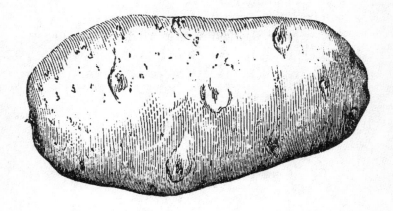

LOCAL YOKEL

By H.E. Dudeney

A stranger out walking came across a local yokel sitting on a wall. He wanted to ask him directions but thought he would test out the yokel's intelligence by asking him a simple question.

'What day of the week is it my good man?' asked the stranger.

Without hesitation the yokel gave the following answer:

'When the day after tomorrow is yesterday, today will be as far from Sunday as today was from Sunday when the day before yesterday was tomorrow.'

What day of the week was it?

CENTURY PUZZLE

Insert the numbers 1–9 inclusive, once each only, into the calculation to arrive at the answer 100.

$$(\quad - \quad) + \quad + \quad - \quad - \quad - \quad = 1\ 0\ 0$$

ANAGRAM SING SONG

All anagrams of well-known Victorian song titles.

Carol:	ACKNOWLEDGE SO SING
Scottish Song:	GAY AND SULLEN
Song/Nursery Rhyme:	GILD ONE LOCK
Scottish Song:	ON COLD HOLM
Marching Song:	RETIRED HIGHEST BRAINS
Folk Song:	NICE EXPLOSIVE

FRANKENSTEIN'S CREATION

For his latest creation Frankenstein takes a large portion from Gertrude, a slice from the middle of Gwenda, a piece from Hermione and a small part from Bessy. After he has put them all together what does Frankenstein call his new creation?

ANAGRAM PHRASES

Each phrase in quotation marks is an anagram of another word. The solution bears some relationship to the original.

'EMIT GRUNT'   THROUGH   'MOUTH CASE'

YARBOROUGH

A hand in bridge in which all 13 cards are a nine or below is called a Yarborough, after the second Earl of Yarborough (d.1897), who frequently bet 1000 to 1 against the dealing of such a hand.

What, however, are the actual odds against such a hand? Was the noble lord onto a good thing?

THE HANDS
OF THE CLOCK

How many times does the long hand of the clock pass the short hand between midnight one day and midnight the following day? As both hands are together at the starting time of midnight this does not count as a pass.

GEOGRAPHICAL PERPLEXITY

A certain island is situated between England and France, and yet that island is further from France than England is. How can this be so?

PAINTING THE LAMPPOSTS

By H.E. Dudeney

Tim and Pat were engaged by the local authority to paint lampposts in a certain street. Tim arrived first and had painted three on the south side when Pat turned up and pointed out that Tim's contract was to paint the north side. So Tim started afresh on the north and Pat continued on the south. When Pat had finished his side he went across the street and painted six posts for Tim and then the job was finished. Which man painted the more lampposts and by how many? There was an equal number of lampposts on each side.

DOUBLE DIGITS

In this multiplication sum each letter stands for a different digit; in other words each of the digits 0–9 occurs twice.

Can you complete the sum?

```
      G H A
      F F B
    ───────
      H G D
    P J C
  P J C
  ─────────
  B K K A D
```

REBUS POETRY

Inscribe an M above a line,
Then write an E below.
The flower you seek is hung so fine,
It sways when breezes blow.

STRIKE OUT THE DOTS

Put the point of your pencil on one of the black dots and without lifting your pencil from the paper strike out all the dots with fourteen continuous straight strokes, ending at the second black dot.

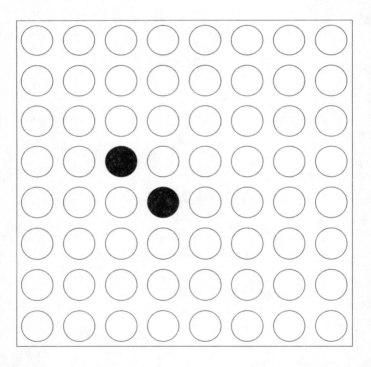

Your straight strokes may be any direction but every change of direction must be on a dot. You may strike out dots more than once on your travels.

SANDS OF TIME

How is it possible to measure 9 minutes when you have only a 4 minute sand glass and a 7 minute sand glass?

TEN WORDS

Complete the ten words with the help of the clues:

TEN _ _ _ _ _ _ _ _ _   Wimbledon competitor (6-6)

_ TEN _ _ _ _ _ _ _ _   Designs made by incisions

_ _ TEN _ _ _ _ _ _ _   Escalating

_ _ _ TEN _ _ _ _ _ _   Very old people

_ _ _ _ TEN _ _ _ _ _   Place of imprisonment

_ _ _ _ _ TEN _ _ _ _   Baptisms

_ _ _ _ _ _ TEN _ _ _   Unhappy

_ _ _ _ _ _ _ TEN _ _   Arranged in order

_ _ _ _ _ _ _ _ TEN _   Occurring occasionally

_ _ _ _ _ _ _ _ _ TEN   Accepted liability

GOLD COIN

Three identical chests of drawers contain two drawers each. Each drawer of chest 'A' contains a gold coin, each drawer of chest 'B' contains a silver coin and chest 'C' has a gold coin in one drawer and silver in the other. You open one of the six drawers at random and find inside a silver coin. What is the probability that the other drawer of the same chest contains a gold coin?

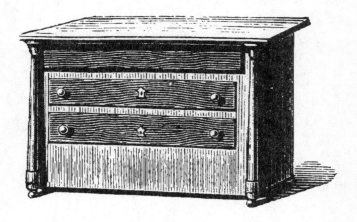

TWO COINS

I have two coins, one is marked George I and one is marked George IV. One is genuine but one is a forgery. Which is the forgery?

ROUND TABLE

Five people are seated at a round table. In how many different ways can the people be seated, where two arrangements in which everybody has the same neighbours are considered the same? For example, consider these arrangements of just four people:

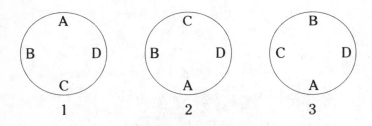

Figures 1 and 2 are considered the same because everyone has the same neighbours, but 1 and 3 and 2 and 3 are different.

MATCHES

Move one match to make this correct:

CROSS-COUNTRY RACE

In the University cross-country race, Algernon was not first, Percival came in after Cuthbert, Clarence was not ahead of Bertie, Algernon was not in front of Percival, Clarence was not fourth or fifth, Bertie was not first.

How did they finish?

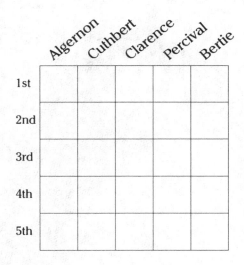

PYRAMID

In the pyramid are ten rooms. You must go into each room once only to spell out a 10-letter word associated with pyramids. You may go into the passage as many times as you wish.

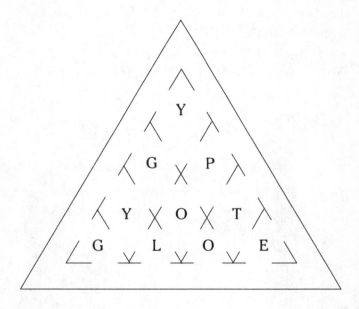

COUNTRY HOUSE

The master of the country house called his servants by their title, i.e. butler, cook, maid, etc. and not politely by their first name, which was standard practice in society in the Victorian era.

One day, a maid took matters into her own hands and said to her master, 'Sir, I demand, I am a maid named Iris.'

What was rather peculiar about that statement?

GOLF

The captain of the golf club had holed out in one. I tried to find out which hole had seen this unusual feat. So, I asked six members; these were their answers:

A said 'The number was made only with straight lines.'

B said 'It had double digits.'

C said 'It had single digits.'

D said 'It had at least one number 1 in it.'

E said 'It was a multiple of three.'

F said 'It was 2 or 8.'

But only one member had told the truth. Which hole was it?

GODDESSES

Can you find the names of these Greek and Roman goddesses? The words run clockwise or anti-clockwise.

Greek goddess of springs and fountains.

Roman goddess of spring flowers.

PALINDROME

Rearrange the pairs of letters and symbols to form a palindrome (reads the same backwards).

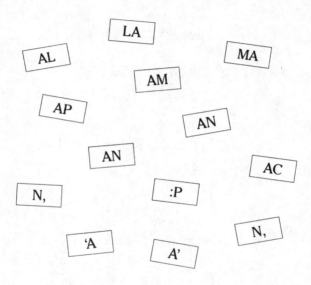

Clue: 'You should take your hat off to George W. Goethals who links seas together.'

WATER LILY

BY LONGFELLOW, THE POET

A water lily stands 10 inches above the surface of the water. If it were pulled over until the head touched the surface it would disappear at a point 21 inches from where it was originally.

How deep is the lake at that point?

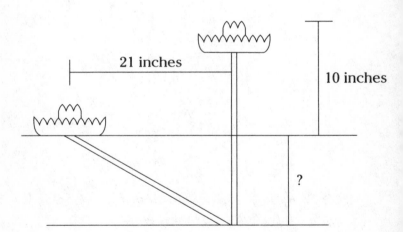

RIVER CROSSING

By Lewis Carroll

Three men with their wives wish to cross a river in a boat only large enough to hold two people. No man must leave his wife on either bank or in the boat unless by herself or in the company of women alone.

How did they do it?

BLYTH'S PARADOX

Spinner A always scores 3.
Spinner B scores 2, 4 or 6.
   probability ·56, ·22, ·22
Spinner C scores 1 or 5.
   probability ·51, ·49

In a two-handed game, which spinner should you choose?
In a three-handed game, which spinner should you choose?

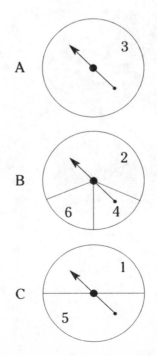

MARS

By Sam Lloyd

Here is a map of old waterways and ancient cities recently discovered on Mars.

Start at the south, City T, and see if you can spell out a complete English sentence, by making a tour of all 20 cities, visiting each city once and returning to T.

When this puzzle was shown in a magazine competition it aroused great interest. More than 50,000 readers reported 'There is no possible way' but it is a simple puzzle.

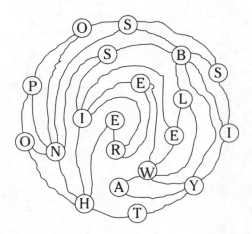

LEWIS CARROLL

A riddle in which the answer is a 6-letter word.

> A monument – men all agree –
> am I in all sincerity,
> half cat, half hindrance made.
> If head and tail removed should be,
> then most of all you strengthen me;
> replace my head, then stand you see
> on which my tail is laid.

PALINDROME

Find this witty saying which is also a palindrome (words).

DOUBLET IV

Change Cain to Abel in nine moves.

C A I N

_ _ _ _

_ _ _ _

_ _ _ _

_ _ _ _

_ _ _ _

_ _ _ _

_ _ _ _

_ _ _ _

_ _ _ _

A B E L

Make a 4-letter word each time.

SAYING

This well known saying has had all of its vowels removed.

Can you replace them?

PPLNG LSSHS SSHLD N'TTHR WSTNS

GROUPS

There are many names of groups of animals, birds, fish and even people. These have been mixed up.

Can you sort them out?

TIDING	OF HUNTERS
SKULK	OF FORESTERS
STALK	OF BADGERS
CLOUD	OF STARLINGS
POD	OF OWLS
MORBIDITY	OF MAGPIES
MURMURATION	OF WHALES
PARLIAMENT	OF FRIARS
BLAST	OF MAJORS
COLONY	OF SEAFOWL

BITS AND PIECES

Here are a set of adjacent letters removed from English words.

UFA

CYT

YRR

WKW

YX

ICICO

RABA

NO VOWELS

Can you find ten 5-letter words in the honeycomb?
Words can be found by following adjacent letters
and letters may be used more than once in a word.

Example: CYSTS

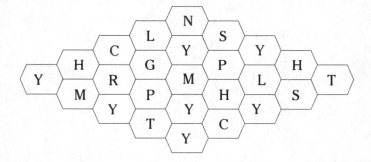

VICTORIAN
WORD SEARCH

All of the words are not now in general use.
Find the words in straight lines, backward, forward
or diagonal. Every letter is used more than once.

J	O	R	E	T	T	E	G
A	K	F	O	R	F	E	X
Z	D	C	A	P	O	N	A
Y	O	D	I	M	P	I	S
Z	G	U	L	R	N	S	A
I	F	A	T	A	R	R	M
F	A	N	F	A	N	E	A
N	O	R	O	M	A	I	D

Clues:
1. A Danish axe
2. A compound of syrup and mulberry juice for a sore throat
3. A hangman
4. A miner
5. A wig
6. A pet dog
7. A pair of scissors
8. The bitter vetch
9. A false god
10. Scottish form of own
11. 8 square yards
12. Alternative spelling of fizz
13. Bird cut into small pieces
14. New Zealand tree
15. Dimples
16. A rose

HONEYCOMB

Find ten or more birds by travelling through the hexagons to adjacent letters. Letters may be used more than once in each word.

NUMBER RHYME

If my three were a four,
and my one were a three,
what I am would be nine less
than half what I'd be.

I'm only three digits,
Just three in a row,
so what in the world must I be?
Do you know?

LAND

A man leaves the piece of land below to his four sons with instructions that it should be divided into four equal pieces each of the same area and all of the same shape as the original piece of land.

How can this be done?

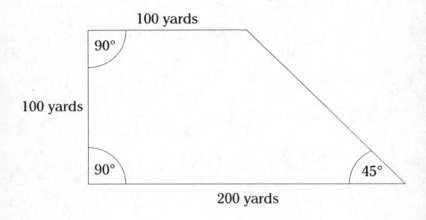

SHARKS

By Lewis Carroll

1. No shark ever doubts that it is well fitted out.

2. A fish that cannot dance a minuet is contemptible.

3. No fish is quite certain that it is well fitted out unless it has three rows of teeth.

4. All fishes, except sharks, are kind to children.

5. No heavy fish can dance a minuet.

6. A fish with three rows of teeth is not to be despised.

What is the conclusion to be reached?

THE CARPENTER'S APPRENTICE

The lad had to repair a hole in the timber floor which was 2 feet wide and 12 feet long.

He was given a board which was 3 feet wide and 8 feet long.

He had to completely cover the hole but only cut the board into two pieces.

How did he do it?

12 feet

| |
| Hole |

2 feet

8 feet

| |
| Board |

3 feet

HUNGRY GOAT

A farmer owns a field shaped in a circle whose area is one hectare. A goat is tethered on the circumference.

What length of rope is required in order for the goat to graze over half of the area of the field?

Goat •————————————— Rope —————————————• Stake

x   y

x = y

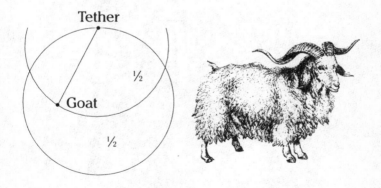

AGES

'When Gwen is twice as old as Dean,
Then I shall be just 17.
But Gwendoline was 23
When Dean was twice as old as me.'
That's what Bill said.

So tell us then,
How old he was when Dean was ten?

CUSTOMS

Two wine merchants arrive at the gates of Paris. One has 64 and the other 20 barrels of wine. Since they have not enough money to pay the custom duties, the first pays 40 francs and 5 barrels of wine. The second pays 2 barrels of wine but receives 40 francs change.

What is the value of each barrel of wine and what is the duty payable?

91

CENSUS-TAKER

An ancient activity in Victorian times was a door-to-door census-taking. A census-taker called at a house in a village, knocked at the door and said to a villager, 'Mr Jones I require the ages of your three daughters.'

'Well,' said Mr Jones, 'if you multiply their ages together you will get a total of 72 and if you add together their ages, a total that will equal the number of my house.'

The census-taker could see the number of the house but he said, 'That is insufficient information.'

'Well,' said Mr Jones, 'my youngest daughter has a dog with a wooden leg.'

'Thank you,' said the census-taker, 'I have sufficient information now.'

How did that work?

PIRATES

Three pirates, One Eye, Long John and Peg Leg, were gambling with pieces of gold. All the winnings were piled up on the table.

One Eye said, 'I have won ½' and took a large handful or two. Long John said, 'I have won ⅓' and took a handful. Peg Leg said, 'I have won ⅙' and took a small handful.

One Eye said, 'I have taken too much' and returned a half. Long John said, 'I have taken too much' and returned a third. Peg Leg said, 'I have taken too much' and returned a sixth.

The money on the table was then shared out equally and they had 42 pieces each.

One Eye said, 'I now have ½ of the total originally.'

Long John said, 'I now have ⅓ of the total originally.'

Peg Leg said, 'I now have ⅙ of the total originally.'

How much was on the table originally?

COUNTER

A bag contains one counter, either black or white. A white counter is put in, a counter is drawn out which proves to be white. What is now the chance of drawing a white counter?

HORSE RACING

There were 13 horses in the race. I wished to know the winner so I asked my friends which horse had won.

> Cecil said, 'It was an odd number.'
> Bertie said, 'It was a prime number.'
> Clarence said, 'It was an even number.'
> Percival said, 'It was a single digit.'
> Cuthbert said, 'It was a square number.'
> Claude said, 'It had a zero in it.'

The number 1 is not considered to be a prime number. Square numbers would be 1, 4 and 9. But only one had told the truth.

Which number had won?

CREATURES

Kneel in the kayak grasping the boat, but don't wrench the bullion or scowl at the chart. Behind the taped and sealed planter is a benevolent collier. The foxglove is in the bath.

Find sixteen creatures in the narrative.

SQUARES AND TRIANGLES

Take eight matches and with them create two squares and four triangles.

DAUGHTERS

A man had four daughters when he died. His eldest daughter was 4 years older than his second daughter, who was 4 years older than his third daughter, who was 4 years older than his fourth daughter, who was half the age of the eldest daughter.

How old were the four daughters?

FARMERS

Farmer Turnip said to Farmer Wheat, 'If you sell me seven acres of your land, I'll own twice as much land as you.' But Farmer Wheat said to Farmer Turnip, 'If you sell me seven acres of your land, I'll have just as much land as you.'

How much land did each farmer have?

SERIES

What are the next two letters in this series?

D E J A F E M A A P M A J U J U _ _

RATS

If seven cats kill seven rats in 7 minutes, how many would be needed to kill one hundred rats in 50 minutes?

TRAVELLERS

Two travellers spend from 12 o'clock to 6 o'clock walking along a level road, up a hill and back again. Their pace is 4 mph on the level, 3 mph uphill, and 6 mph downhill.

How far do they walk and at what time do they reach the top of the hill?

FOOTMEN

By Lewis Carroll

1. All of the human race, except my footmen, have a certain amount of common sense.

2. No one who lives on barley sugar can be anything but a mere baby.

3. None but a hopscotch player knows what real happiness is.

4. No mere baby has a grain of common sense.

5. No engine driver ever plays hopscotch.

6. No footman of mine is ignorant of what true happiness is.

What is the conclusion to be reached?

TRAINS

Two travellers starting at the same time went opposite ways around a circular railway. Trains start each way every 15 minutes, the easterly ones going round in 3 hours and the westerly in 2 hours.

How many trains pass each other before the two travellers meet at the terminus?

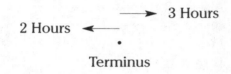

3 Hours

2 Hours

Terminus

CASINO

The casino manager wished to check the bias on the roulette wheel, so he asked six of his croupiers to report back to him at the end of the week with the number on the wheel which had been most successful.

The wheel consisted of 36 numbers 1 to 36 with no zero.

These were the 6 answers:
A said, 'It was even.'
B said, 'It was odd.'
C said, 'It was prime.'
D said, 'It was square.'
E said, 'It had at least one 2 in it.'
F said, 'It was a single digit.'

The number 1 is not considered to be a prime number. A square number would be 1, 4, 9, 16, 25 or 36. But two had lied.

Which number was it?

SACKS

The corn chandler had five sacks of corn.

Sacks
1+2 together weighed 12 lbs;
2+3 together weighed 13.5 lbs;
3+4 together weighed 11.5 lbs;
4+5 together weighed 8 lbs;
1+3+5 together weighed 16 lbs.

What is the weight of each sack?

STATION

In the railway station buffet two girls consumed the following:

Priscilla   1 glass of lemonade
                3 sandwiches
                7 biscuits
                cost 1s 2d

Gloria   1 glass of lemonade
                4 sandwiches
                10 biscuits
                cost 1s 5d

What would be the cost of:
        1 glass of lemonade
        1 sandwich
        1 biscuit
        ?

GARDEN

A walled garden 30 feet square had a 2-foot pathway bounded by a hedge. (For the purposes of this puzzle the hedge has no width.) This pathway spiralled into the centre. How far would you have to walk to reach the centre?

30 feet

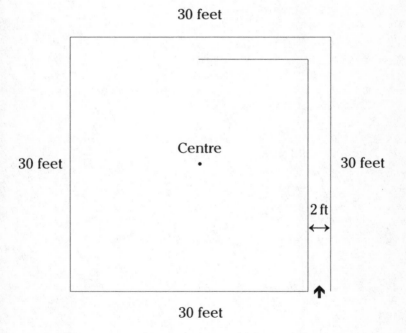

30 feet

Centre
•

30 feet

2 ft

30 feet

DOUBLET V

Change river to shore in eleven moves.

R I V E R

_ _ _ _ _

_ _ _ _ _

_ _ _ _ _

_ _ _ _ _

_ _ _ _ _

_ _ _ _ _

_ _ _ _ _

_ _ _ _ _

_ _ _ _ _

_ _ _ _ _

S H O R E

FLUTES

One day a new consignment of flutes arrived for the orchestra in which there were eleven flautists.

The first flautist took one-eleventh of the flutes plus one-eleventh of a flute. The second flautist took one-tenth of the remainder plus one-tenth of a flute. The third flautist took one-ninth of the remainder plus one-ninth of a flute and so on. The next to last took half of what remained plus half a flute.

I was last and when I saw how many that they had left me, I resigned because everybody else got twice as many flutes as I did.

How many flutes were in the consignment?

HEXAGRAM

Rearrange the letters to form the names of six animals. Transfer the arrowed letters into the key anagram and then rearrange the letters to form a seventh animal.

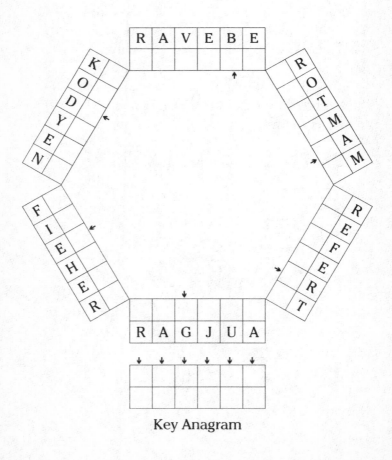

Key Anagram

FARMERS

Two farmers, Thistle and Corncob, were partners and had a stock of cattle. Business was not too good so they decided to go to market, sell the cattle and buy sheep with the proceeds. For each cow sold they received a number of guineas equal to the number of cows that they had. For instance, if they had 20 cows they would have 20 guineas for each one. With this money they purchased a number of sheep which they shared. The sheep cost 10 guineas each, but there was some money left over, less than 10 guineas, so with this money they purchased a goat.

As they had bought an odd number of sheep, Farmer Thistle said, 'I will keep the odd sheep and you can have the goat.' Farmer Corncob said, 'That's not fair, a sheep is worth more than a goat.'

'All right,' said Farmer Thistle, 'I will give you four chickens as well.'

What was the value of the four chickens?

RIDDLE

By Lewis Carroll

Dreaming of apples on a wall,
And dreaming often, dear,
I dreamed that, if I counted all,
How many would appear?

How many?

PRISONER

I wished to know in which cell the prisoner was held so I asked six prison warders. I knew that there were 20 cells in the prison.

These were their answers:
A said, 'It was odd.'
B said, 'It was even.'
C said, 'It was double digits.'
D said, 'It had at least one number 1 in it.'
E said, 'It was a multiple of 3.'
F said, 'It was between 6 and 13.'

But one had lied. Which cell was it?

COMMON

What do these words have in common?

DEFENDING

CALMNESS

SIGHING

CANOPY

STUMBLE

TRIANGLE

Take nine matches and arrange them like this:

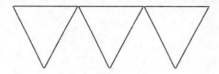

Now move three matches and create five triangles.

DOUBLE PALINDROMES

Find two palindromes in the target.

One has seven words; the other has nine words.

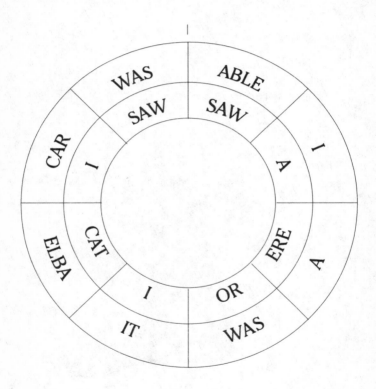

STUCK UP

Find two 5-letter words by moving along the lines and into each circle once only.

Clue: stuck up, rhyming

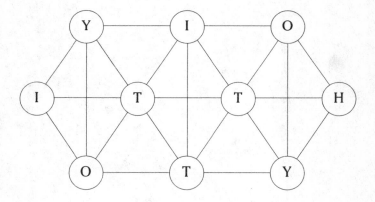

ABRACADABRA

How many different ways of spelling ABRACADABRA can you find?

```
                A
              B   B
            R   R   R
          A   A   A   A
        C   C   C   C   C
      A   A   A   A   A   A
    D   D   D   D   D   D   D
  A   A   A   A   A   A   A   A
B   B   B   B   B   B   B   B   B
R   R   R   R   R   R   R   R   R   R
A   A   A   A   A   A   A   A   A   A   A
```

GROUPS

There are many names of groups of animals, birds, fish and even people. These have been mixed up.

Can you sort them out?

SORD	OF ROOKS
BLUSH	OF CURS
DESERT	OF SWANS
COVERT	OF MALLARD
CONVOCATION	OF LIONS
HERD	OF HERMITS
COWARDICE	OF BOYS
PRIDE	OF LAPWING
OBSERVANCE	OF EAGLES
BUILDING	OF COOTS

MAGIC SQUARE

Each word is repeated across and down, i.e.

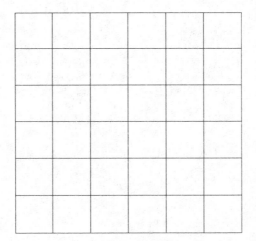

R	E	D
E	R	E
D	E	N

Clues in no particular order:

1. Give help
2. One at a time
3. Polishing cloth
4. Secret meetings
5. Choose
6. Fireplaces

PAIRS

There are 21 words which can be paired up to make 10 pairs with one word left over.

Can you find that word?

duckling   manners   stamp
blossom   cherry   beaufort
table   rabbit   village
warren   green   winter
yellow   almond   chested
hollow   streak   ugly
scale   sleepy   barrel

BITS AND PIECES

Here are sets of adjacent letters removed from eight English words. Some are hyphenated.

N X

C K N

O O K K E E

H A N H

L L S C

C H Y D

Z Z O R

Can you reconstitute them?

MAGIC SQUARE

Each word is repeated across and down, i.e.

R	E	D
E	R	E
D	E	N

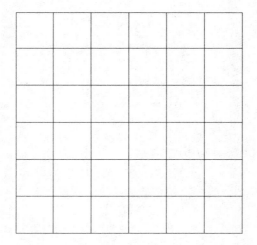

Clues in no particular order:

1. Flower
2. Trigonometrical
3. Stage plays

4. Come to notice
5. Of small particles
6. Retreat

WORDS

What have these words in common?

ASPIRATED

GRANGERS

PRELATES

SWINGERS

CHASTENS

LETTERS

Form a word from the letters A B C D E F G I using each letter once.

The word is hyphenated.

PAIRING

Each word in list B has two possible pairings in list A.
Each word in list A has two possible pairings in list B.

List A	List B
penny	water
fence	coin
ring	sugar
moidore	pale
doughnut	epee
white	torns
sword	gold
beet	black
sea	root
tap	fish

VICTORIAN
WORD SEARCH

All of the words are not now in general use.

Find the words in straight lines, backward, forward or diagonal. Every letter is used some more than once.

Clues

1. A stick used in the bedroom to stop the bedclothes from slipping
2. A dagger
3. Name given to a group of ducks
4. A fat, unwieldy woman
5. Oatmeal pottage boiled in beer dregs
6. A gooseherd
7. A gold coin
8. A place for drying herrings
9. Lard
10. A pointed hammer for trimming slate
11. A Portuguese coin
12. A pillar
13. Sheep's perspiration
14. A tall conical hat
15. A type of yak
16. A drainage canal

D	R	O	W	S	E	N	F
D	R	O	E	A	J	U	F
R	E	A	H	S	Z	A	A
A	Y	X	L	Z	E	D	T
Z	A	P	O	E	E	E	S
Z	T	C	P	P	S	K	D
O	K	A	S	O	I	A	E
G	N	Y	L	E	D	A	B

KNIGHT'S MOVE

Find the starting point then, using the knight's move in chess, work out the message.

Time	The	Be	Ahead	Friday
Wishing	Man	His	Employee	He'll
Of	On	As	Were	Of
A	It	Beware	Wednesday	Heralded

	✕		✕	
✕				✕
		Kn		
✕				✕
	✕		✕	

Knight's Move

TRICKY

Re-arrange the letters,
O O U S W T D N E J R
to spell just one word.

CHARLOTTE

Charlotte is 13 years old. Her father Montague is 40 years old. How many years ago was Charlotte's father four times as old as Charlotte?

ARAB

An arab came to the river side,
with a donkey bearing an obelisk.
But he did not venture to ford the tide,
for he had too good an   *   .

What is the missing word?

HOUSE NUMBER

I wished to know my friend's house number.
I knew that it was between 1 and 50. When I
asked him he said, 'Well if you can find the
answer to these three questions, then you will
know the number.'

1. 'Is it odd?'
2. 'Is it prime?'
3. 'Is it a cube?' (e.g., numbers 1, 8, 27 are the
   cubes of 1, 2, 3).

I then knew the number; what was it? And what
were the answers?

The number 1 is not considered to be a prime number.

BARREL

'This barrel of rum is more than half full,' said Bert.
'No it's not,' said Alf, 'it's less than half full.'

*How could they tell it one way or the other without
any measuring devices?*

ANAGRAMS

These are all anagrams of animals.

1. corona

2. paroled

3. retirer

4. lesions

5. someday

6. alpines

7. orchestra

8. californian (two words)

MONTH

I wished to know the month of the garden fete so I asked six of my friends. These were their answers.

> A said, 'It began with the letter J.'
> B said, 'It had only 5 letters in its name.'
> C said, 'It had 30 days in its month.'
> D said, 'It had 31 days in its month.'
> E said, 'It had 3 vowels in its month.'
> F said, 'It ended in y.'

But half had lied. Which month was it?

OCTAHEDRAL DICE

A casino had invented eight-sided dice, numbered 1 to 8. The gambler should throw a pair of these dice and try to score exactly six.

The casino paid odds of 10 to 1. Was this a fair bet?

CHILDREN

A man has nine children, born at regular intervals. The sum of the squares of their ages is equal to the square of his own age.

What are the ages of the children?

MURDERER IN THE MANSION

The owner of the mansion had been murdered. The visitors to the mansion were Allen, Bixby and Crain.

1. The murderer, who was one of the three visitors, arrived at the mansion later than at least one of the other two visitors.

2. A detective, who was one of the three visitors, arrived at the mansion earlier than at least one of the other two visitors.

3. The detective arrived at midnight.

4. Neither Allen nor Bixby arrived at the mansion after midnight.

5. The earlier arriver of Bixby and Crain was not the detective.

6. The later arrival of Allen and Crain was not the murderer.

Who was the murderer?

THE VILLAGE HALL

Out of 100 ladies attending the church fete,
85 had a white handbag;
75 had black shoes;
60 carried an umbrella;
90 wore a ring.

How many ladies must have had all four items?

POEMS

BY LEWIS CARROLL

1. No interesting poems are unpopular among people of real taste.
2. No modern poetry is free from affectation.
3. All your poems are on the subject of soap bubbles.
4. No affected poetry is popular among people of real taste.
5. No ancient poem is on the subject of soap bubbles.

What is the conclusion?

SPIDER'S WEB

In an alcove was a spider's web.

The arc of the web is exactly one quarter of a circle and 20 inches long.

What is the area of the web?

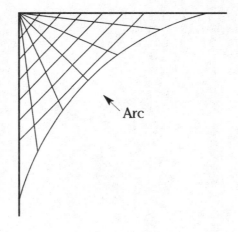

Arc

ANSWERS

RANK AND FILE *page 5*
301 soldiers

SOLITAIRE *page 6*

1.	9 to 1	17.	28 to 30
2.	7 to 9	18.	33 to 25
3.	10 to 8	19.	18 to 30
4.	21 to 7	20.	31 to 33
5.	7 to 9	21.	33 to 25
6.	22 to 8	22.	26 to 24
7.	8 to 10	23.	16 to 18
8.	6 to 4	24.	23 to 25
9.	1 to 9	25.	25 to 11
10.	18 to 6	26.	6 to 18
11.	3 to 11	27.	13 to 11
12.	20 to 18	28.	18 to 6
13.	18 to 6	29.	9 to 11
14.	30 to 18	30.	11 to 3
15.	27 to 25	31.	3 to 1
16.	24 to 26		

DOUBLET I *page 7*

```
B  L  U  E
G  L  U  E
G  L  U  T
G  O  U  T
P  O  U  T
P  O  R  T
P  A  R  T
P  A  N  T
P  I  N  T
P  I  N  K
```

WORD PLAY *page 7*
1. Time and tide wait for no man.
2. Birds of a feather flock together.
3. A rolling stone gathers no moss.

NINE IN A ROW *page 8*

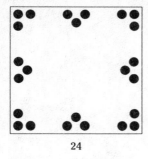

24

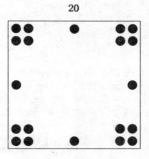

20

RELATIVELY SPEAKING *page 9*
His son

FORTY-FIVE *page 9*

$$8 + 2 = 10$$
$$12 - 2 = 10$$
$$5 \times 2 = 10$$
$$\underline{20 \div 2 = 10}$$
$$45$$

CASK OF WINE *page 10*

8 GALLON	3 GALLON	5 GALLON
8	0	0
3	0	5
3	3	2
6	0	2
6	2	0
1	2	5
1	3	4
4	0	4

CUPS AND SAUCERS *page 11*
The larger cup weighed 6 ounces, the smaller cup 4 ounces and the
saucer 2 ounces.

DIVISION SUM *page 12*

```
315 )  86625 ( 275
       630
       2362
       2205
        1575
        1575
        . . . .
```

BOYS AND GIRLS *page 13*
Follow this route to spell out:
ALICE, CLARENCE, POLLY, AUBREY, FELICITY, HENRY, EDWINA,
DERMOT, KATIE, HUGO, MADELINE.

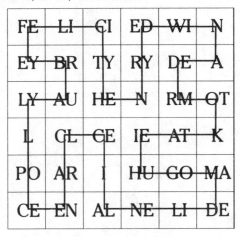

FOUR INTEGERS *page 14*
A = 9, B = 6, C = 3, D = 1.
CABA = 3969 (63^2), DCBA = 1369 (37^2), DACB = 1936 (44^2).

CATCHING A THIEF *page 15*
30 steps. The constable took 30 steps in the same time the thief took
48, which added to his start of 27, would have carried him 75 steps.
This distance is exactly equal to 30 steps of the constable.

FILLING A BATH *page 16*
2 mins 24 seconds

$$\frac{1}{6} + \frac{1}{2} - \frac{1}{4} = 0.416$$

Hot takes 6 mins to fill. Cold takes 2 mins to fill.
It takes 4 mins to empty

Add hot and cold reciprocals ⅙ = .166
                                    ½ = .500
                                         ‾‾‾‾
                                         .666
Subtract empty reciprocal ¼ = .250
                         Total = .416

The bath fills in $\frac{1}{0.416}$ minutes

= 2·40 minutes or 2 minutes 24 seconds

BEHEADMENT RIDDLE *page 16*
WHEAT
  HEAT
   EAT

COUNTERS *page 17*

Move 1: 2 and 3 to 13 and 14	Move 4: 6 and 7 to 10 and 11
Move 2: 5 and 6 to 2 and 3	Move 5: 12 and 13 to 6 and 7
Move 3: 10 and 11 to 5 and 6	Move 6: 1 and 2 to 12 and 13

FOWL CALCULATIONS *page 17*
Two ducks and three hens equal three pheasants. It follows, therefore, that £4 represents the price of four pheasants or £1 each. This leaves a balance of £3 as he only bought one pheasant. However, if three hens cost the same as two ducks, each lot must cost 30 shillings (half of £3). Each duck, therefore, costs 15 shillings and each hen 10 shillings.

		£.	s.	d.
To summarise:	1 pheasant =	£1.	0.	0
	2 ducks =	£1.	10.	0
	3 hens =	£1.	10.	0

(20 shillings = £1 in old money)

VICTORIAN ANAGRAMS *page 18*
CHRISTIANITY
NO TRESPASSING
KNIGHTS OF THE ROUND TABLE
FLORENCE NIGHTINGALE

THE LINOLEUM PUZZLE *page 19*
Cut along the thick lines and assemble as shown.

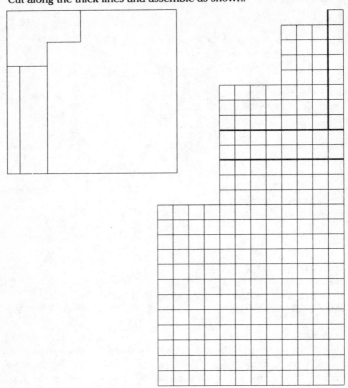

GRANDMOTHER'S BIRTHDAY *page 20*
5

LITTLE TOMMY TITTLETAT *page 20*
There are two Ts in 'All of that'.

QUIET VERONICA *page 21*
QUEEN VICTORIA   PRINCE ALBERT   BENJAMIN DISRAELI
ALEXANDER GRAHAM BELL   CHARLOTTE BRONTË
CHARLES DARWIN   DAVID LIVINGSTONE   MICHAEL FARADAY
SIR HENRY IRVING   GEORGE BERNARD SHAW

PHALANX *page 22*

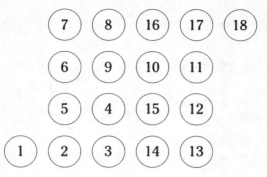

EIGHT EIGHTS *page 23*
```
8 8 8
  8 8
    8
    8
    8
1000
```

AGES TEASER *page 23*
Edward is 48

MAGIC PRIME *page 24*

103	79	37
7	73	139
109	67	43

RING THE BELL *page 25*

7 people rang the bell	7 × £10	=	£	70.	0.	0
49 people scored 95	49 × 10s	=	£	24.	10.	0
44 people scored 90	44 × 2/6d	=	£	5.	10.	0
			£100.		0.	0

TOMATOES *page 26*

7

To his first parishioner	$3.5 + 0.5 = 4$
To his second parishioner	$1.5 + 0.5 = 2$
To his third parishioner	$0.5 + 0.5 = 1$

REBUS CONUNDRUM *page 27*

Conundrum: What is black and white and re[a]d all over?
Answer: A newspaper

MIXED FRACTION *page 28*

$$15 = 3 + \left(\frac{\frac{8952}{746}}{1} \right)$$

THREE ANIMALS *page 28*

PANTHER, ANTELOPE, LLAMA

THE TWO YOUNG ENTREPRENEURS *page 29*

By going into partnership Amy was now getting a penny from each of 120 sales instead of 100 and made 20 pence more than the first day. Matthew was also taking a penny each from 120 sales but had made 150 sales at a penny each the first day so was 30 pence down. Their customers bought 600 bags for 240 pence on the second day whereas for the same 600 bags on the first day they had paid 250 pence. Amy and the customers were the beneficiaries at the expense of Matthew.

PALINDROMES *page 30*

1. NAME NO ONE MAN
2. DO GEESE SEE GOD?
3. NO LEMONS, NO MELON
4. MADAM, IN EDEN, I'M ADAM
5. ANNE, I VOTE MORE CARS RACE ROME TO VIENNA
6. DOC, NOTE; I DISSENT, A FAST NEVER PREVENTS A FATNESS, I DIET ON COD

THE MAGIC HEXAGON *page 31*

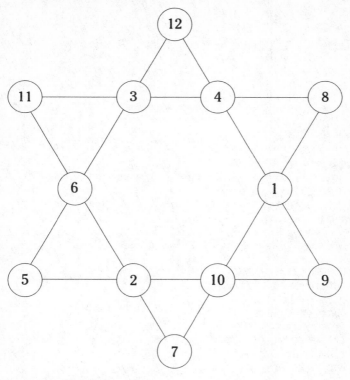

THE URBAN RIDDLE *page 32*
Rome, Ely, Paris, Chester
Line One: NEA (R O ME) N
Line Two: AR (E LY) ING
Line Three: U (P A RIS) EN
Line Four: AR (CHES TER) RACES

STRIKING CLOCK *page 32*
22 seconds

THREE CLASSICS *page 33*
1. ONE WORD IS AN ANAGRAM OF NEW DOOR
2. BAYONET
3. SOMERSAULT

DOUBLET II *page 34*

```
L  O  A  F
L  E  A  F
D  E  A  F
D  E  A  R
D  E  E  R
D  Y  E  R
D  Y  E  S
E  Y  E  S
E  V  E  S
E  V  E  N
O  V  E  N
```

TALL TREE STORY *page 34*
Still 3.5 feet. It is the top part of the tree that grows. The trunk only gets bigger in circumference.

BACKWARDS AND FORWARDS *page 35*
The man walks for 9 miles at 4 mph. which takes 2.25 hours. The dog, therefore, runs for 2.25 hours at 9 mph. and covers 20.25 miles.

CHILDREN'S CAKES *page 36*
A CHRISTMAS CAROL
DAVID COPPERFIELD
THE OLD CURIOSITY SHOP
OLIVER TWIST
GREAT EXPECTATIONS
NICHOLAS NICKLEBY

SIMPLE ADDITION *page 37*
11 o'clock plus 2 hours = 1 o'clock
9 o'clock plus 5 hours = 2 o'clock

STRANGE SUBTRACTION *page 37*
F̸ I V E̸ = I V

OLD PALS *page 38*

The possibilities are:

	OLDEST CHILD	YOUNGEST CHILD
1.	GIRL	GIRL
2.	GIRL	BOY
3.	BOY	GIRL
4.	BOY	BOY

By answering 'yes' to the second question, Ernest eliminated cases 3 and 4 and in the remaining cases both are girls in half the remaining two possibilities. By answering 'yes' to the alternative question, Ernest has eliminated case 4 only and in one out of three of the remaining possibilities both are girls.

MAGIC WORD SQUARE *page 39*

1 C	2 I	3 R	4 C	5 L	6 E
2 I	C	A	R	U	S
3 R	A	R	E	S	T
4 C	R	E	A	T	E
5 L	U	S	T	R	E
6 E	S	T	E	E	M

THE EIFFEL TOWER *page 40*
984 feet

GRANDPA'S PARTY *page 41*
My grandfather is seventy-two years old.
I am twenty-two years old.
Sixty grandsons received invitations.

PENNIES *page 42*
Because there is one more of them.
In old currency   1888 pennies = £ 7. 17. 4
                      1887 pennies = £ 7. 17. 3

TWO FRACTIONS *page 42*
$$\frac{35}{70} + \frac{148}{296} = 1$$

TEN TREES *page 43*
Four different ways:

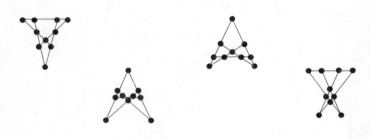

WAS IT A CAT I SAW? *page 44*
138,384
There are 372 ways forward. As the phrase is palindromic there are as many ways backwards. The square of 372 gives a total of 138,384 ways, all different.

THE FIVE PENNIES *page 45*
There are thirty-two possible ways for the coins to fall:
A. FIVE HEADS (one way)
B. FIVE TAILS (one way)
C. FOUR HEADS AND ONE TAIL (five ways)
D. FOUR TAILS AND ONE HEAD (five ways)
E. THREE HEADS AND TWO TAILS (ten ways)
F. THREE TAILS AND TWO HEADS (ten ways)
Of these, A, B, C and D (12 ways) are favourable, but the other twenty ways, E and F, are not. The chances, therefore, are twelve chances out of thirty-two, or three chances out of eight.

TREASURE TRAIL *page 46*

Visit the squares in the following order:

39	51	3	37	14	34	43	12
45	38	52	18	42	8	13	36
17	1	33	7	28	41	35	22
58	62	50	40	2	32	55	53
49	24	16	4	44	20	T	31
61	59	25	9	21	29	48	56
47	15	5	27	30	11	19	63
10	26	46	57	23	54	6	60

COUNTERS *page 47*

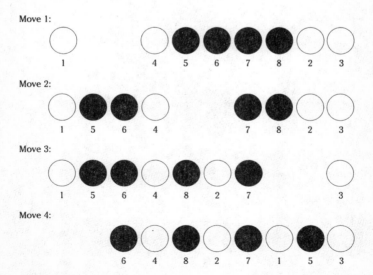

147

DOUBLET III *page 48*

```
R   O   G   U   E
V   O   G   U   E
V   A   G   U   E
V   A   L   U   E
V   A   L   V   E
H   A   L   V   E
H   E   L   V   E
H   E   A   V   E
L   E   A   V   E
L   E   A   S   E
L   E   A   S   T
B   E   A   S   T
```

PIECE OF CHEESE *page 49*
Twenty-two pieces

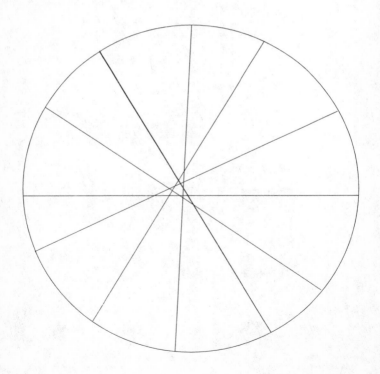

SQUARES *page 50*
YES:

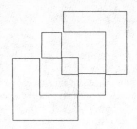

COUNTERFEIT COIN *page 50*
Step A: Weigh 1, 2, 3, 4 against 5, 6, 7, 8
Step B: Weigh 9, 10, 11, 4 against 1, 2, 3, 8
Step C: There are five possibilities.
i)   If the scales were balanced both times, 12 is the counterfeit.
     Weigh it against another to see if it is heavy or light.
ii) If the scales were balanced for Step A but not for Step B, weigh
     9 against 10 to see which tips the same way as in Step B. If they
     balance, 11 is the counterfeit (heavy or light as shown in Step B).
iii) If the scales were balanced for Step B but not Step A, weigh 5
     against 6 to see which tips the same way as in Step A. If they
     balance, 7 is the counterfeit (heavy or light as shown in Step A).
iv) If the scales were off-balance the same way both times, weigh 4
     against another coin. If they balance, the counterfeit is 8 (heavy
     or light as shown in Steps A and B).
v)   If the scales were off-balance in opposite ways in Step A and B,
     weigh 1 against 2 to see which tips as 1, 2, 3 tipped in Step B. If they
     balance, 3 is the counterfeit (heavy or light as shown in Step B).

DOUBLE ACROSTIC *page 51*
M EADO W
A LIB I
R EASO N
C ROW D
H ARAS S

THE BY-ELECTION *page 52*
Add the sum of the three majorities to the total poll of 7396
ie. 7396 + 592 + 794 + 962 = 9744
Now divide by 4 = 2436.
This gives us the number of votes polled by the Liberal.
The votes cast were therefore:
Liberal : 2436
Socialist : 1844
Conservative : 1642
Independent : 1474

BAG OF POTATOES *page 53*
8 lbs

LOCAL YOKEL *page 54*
Sunday
When the day after tomorrow (Tuesday) is 'yesterday', 'today' will be
Wednesday; and when the day before yesterday (Friday) was
'tomorrow', 'today' was Thursday. There are two days between
Thursday and Sunday, and between Sunday and Wednesday.

CENTURY PUZZLE *page 55*
$(7 - 5)^2 + 96 + 8 - 4 - 3 - 1 = 100$

ANAGRAM SING SONG *page 55*
GOOD KING WENCESLAS
AULD LANG SYNE
OLD KING COLE
LOCH LOMOND
THE BRITISH GRENADIERS
I LOVE SIXPENCE

FRANKENSTEIN'S CREATION *page 56*
ERMENTRUDE – HERMIONE, GWENDA, GERTRUDE, BESSY

ANAGRAM PHRASES *page 56*
MUTTERING THROUGH MOUSTACHE

YARBOROUGH *page 57*
In a pack of 52 cards there are 32 cards of nine or below. The chance
that the first card dealt is one of the 32 is $\frac{32}{52}$, the second card $\frac{31}{51}$ ... etc.

The chance of all 13 being favourable is
$$\frac{32}{52} \times \frac{31}{51} \ldots \ldots \ldots \frac{20}{40} \quad \text{or} \quad \frac{1}{1828}.$$
The odds were strongly in Lord Yarborough's favour.

THE HANDS OF THE CLOCK *page 58*
21

GEOGRAPHICAL PERPLEXITY *page 59*
Guernsey is about 26 miles from France, and England is only 21
miles from France between Calais and Dover.

PAINTING THE LAMPPOSTS *page 60*
Pat painted six more posts than Tim, no matter how many lampposts there were.

DOUBLE DIGITS *page 61*
```
    1 7 9
    2 2 4
    7 1 6
  3 5 8
  3 5 8
4 0 0 9 6
```

REBUS POETRY *page 61*
$$\frac{M}{E}$$ (anEMonE)
ANEMONE

STRIKE OUT THE DOTS *page 62*

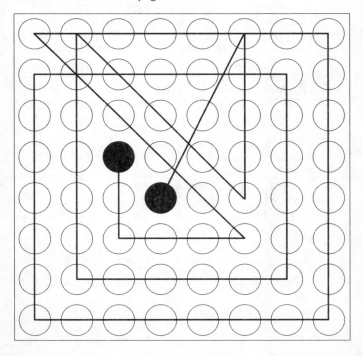

SANDS OF TIME *page 63*
Start them both running at the same time. Turn the 4 minute glass over as soon as it runs out (4 minutes). Turn the 7 minute glass over when that runs out (an extra 3 minutes). At that moment, the 4 minute glass has 1 minute left. Turn it over when that 1 minute is over (plus 1 minute). Then turn the 7 minute glass over, which ran for only 1 minute (plus 1 minute). That makes a total of 9 minutes (4+3+1+1).

TEN WORDS *page 64*
TENNIS-PLAYER STENCILLINGS INTENSIFYING CENTENARIANS
PENITENTIARY CHRISTENINGS DISCONTENTED STRAIGHTENED
INTERMITTENT UNDERWRITTEN

GOLD COIN *page 65*
Knowing that a drawer of either chest 'B' or 'C' has been opened might lead people to believe that the probability is ½. However, as we are dealing with drawers and not chests the answer is ⅓. The three drawers containing silver coins represent equally likely cases, and only one of these is favourable, namely the drawer with the silver coin in chest 'C'. The probability that chest 'C' has been opened is initially ⅓ and remains ⅓ when a drawer has been opened and found to have a silver coin, because gold and silver are distributed identically over drawers and chests.

TWO COINS *page 65*
George I. A coin would not be marked George I because at the time it was produced it would not be known whether there would be a George II.

ROUND TABLE *page 66*
Twelve different ways. Calling the people 1, 2, 3, 4, 5; it is irrelevant where 1 is seated. The remaining four people can be seated in 24 ways (4 × 3 × 2 × 1). However, as left and right are considered the same, the answer is 24 ÷ 2 = 12 different ways.

MATCHES *page 67*
$$Pi = \frac{22}{7}$$

CROSS-COUNTRY RACE *page 68*
1st Cuthbert 2nd Bertie 3rd Clarence 4th Percival 5th Algernon

PYRAMID *page 69*
Egyptology

COUNTRY HOUSE *page 70*
It was a palindrome (It reads the same backwards!)

GOLF *page 71*

	A	B	C	D	E	F
1	✓		✓	✓		
2			✓			✓
3			✓	✓		
4	✓		✓			
5			✓			
6			✓	✓		
7	✓		✓			
8			✓			✓
9			✓	✓		

	A	B	C	D	E	F
10		✓		✓		
11	✓	✓		✓		
12		✓		✓	✓	
13		✓		✓		
14	✓	✓		✓		
15		✓		✓	✓	
16		✓		✓		
17	✓	✓		✓		
18		✓		✓	✓	

A tick means a true answer. Only hole 5 has one ✓ so 5 is the answer.

GODDESSES *page 72*
Arethusa Feronia

PALINDROME *page 73*
'A man, a plan, a canal: panama' Which honours George W Goethals, the engineer who devised the Panama Canal.

WATER LILY *page 74*
17.05 inches
Using theory of chords
$21 \times 21 = 10 \times 44.1$ (441 = 441)
$\frac{54.1}{2} = 27.05 - 10 = 17.05$

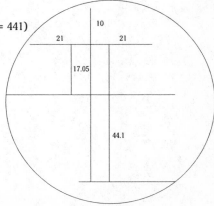

RIVER CROSSING *page 75*

ABC = MEN   abc = WOMEN

	BANK		OTHER SIDE
1.	ABC abc		
2.	ABC	c	ab
3.	ABC	bc	a
4.	ABC		abc
5.	ABC	b	a c
6.	B	b	A C a c
7.	AB	ab	C c
8.		ab	ABC c
9.		abc	ABC
10.		b	ABC a c
11.		bc	ABC a
12.			ABC abc

BLYTH'S PARADOX *page 76*

A beats B 1 × ·56 = ·56
A beats C 1 × ·51 = ·51
B beats C (1 × ·22) + (·22 × ·51) + (·56 × ·51) = ·6178
A is best for 2-handed
A (·56 × ·51) = ·2856
B (·44 × ·51) + (·22 × ·49) = ·3322
C (·49 × ·78) = ·3822
C is best for 3-handed.

MARS *page 77*
That is the answer – 'There is no possible way'

LEWIS CARROLL *page 78*
Tablet

PALINDROME *page 79*
You can cage a swallow, can't you,
but you can't swallow a cage can you?

DOUBLET IV *page 80*

C	A	I	N
C	H	I	N
S	H	I	N
S	P	I	N
S	P	U	N
S	P	U	D
S	P	E	D
A	P	E	D
A	B	E	D
A	B	E	L

SAYING *page 80*

'People in glasshouses shouldn't throw stones.'

GROUPS *page 81*

BLAST	OF	HUNTERS
STALK	OF	FORESTERS
COLONY	OF	BADGERS
MURMURATION	OF	STARLINGS
PARLIAMENT	OF	OWLS
TIDING	OF	MAGPIES
POD	OF	WHALES
SKULK	OF	FRIARS
MORBIDITY	OF	MAJORS
CLOUD	OF	SEAFOWL

BITS AND PIECES *page 82*

manufacture   scythe   pyrrhic   awkward   onyx
silicicolous   contrabassoon

NO VOWELS *page 83*

NYMPH   PYGMY   GYPSY   SYLPH   SHYLY
SLYLY   LYMPH   CRYPT   CYSTS   MYRRH

VICTORIAN WORD SEARCH *page 84*

1. damasax   2. diamoron   3. derrick   4. getter   5. jazy   6. fanfan
7. forfex   8. ers   9. afgod   10. ain   11. fo   12. fiz   13. capon   14.
rata   15. dimp   16. gul

HONEYCOMB *page 85*

THRUSH   SKUA   AUK   KIWI   ROBIN   ROC   IBIS   WREN
EMU   CROW

NUMBER RHYME *page 85*

Half of 'What I'd be' must be a whole number.

'What I'd be' must be an even number.

'What I am' cannot end in 1.

There are four possible arrangements of the three digits.

	(a)	(b)	(c)	(d)
'What I am'	1 ? 3	1 3 ?	3 1 ?	? 1 3
'What I'd be'	3 ? 4	3 4 ?	4 3 ?	? 3 4

'What I am' is 'nine less than half what I'd be',
so ('what I am' + 9) × 2 = 'what I'd be'.
Only A fits the bill and 'what I am' must be 183.

LAND *page 86*

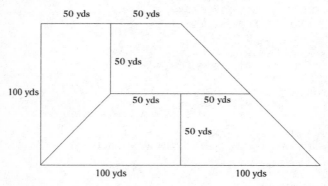

SHARKS *page 87*

'No heavy fish is unkind to children.'

THE CARPENTER'S APPRENTICE *page 88*

HUNGRY GOAT *page 89*

As a proportion of the diameter of the circle. The answer is:

0 · 5 7 9 3 6 4 2 3 6 5 0 9 0 6 0 7 5 8 9 1 4 1 1 6 7 5 5 D -

This number is of course indeterminate and can be carried on to infinity.

AGES *page 90*

Eight

CUSTOMS *page 91*

The value of a barrel is 120 francs and the duty is 10 francs a barrel.

CENSUS-TAKER *page 92*

We must first take the factors of 72.

	Add to find door number	
72 = 1 × 1 × 72		74
1 × 2 × 36		39
1 × 3 × 24		28
1 × 4 × 18		23
1 × 6 × 12		19
1 × 8 × 9		18
2 × 2 × 18		22
2 × 3 × 12		17
2 × 4 × 9		15
2 × 6 × 6		14*
3 × 3 × 8		14*
3 × 4 × 6		13

Now the census-taker should have known the answer as he could see the door number but the door number was 14* so he needed to know whether it was 2 × 6 × 6 or 3 × 3 × 8.

When he knew that there was a younger daughter he knew the answer was 2, 6, 6. That is, there was only one combination total (14) in which there were two possible sets of ages, requiring him to ask for further information, and only one of these had a single 'youngest' daughter (aged 2).

PIRATES *page 93*
282 pieces

	One Eye	Long John	Peg Leg	Total
Taken from original pile	198	78	6	282
Returned to table	(½)	(⅓)	(⅙)	
	99	26	1	126
Retained by pirates	99	52	5	156
Shared out equally	42	42	42	126
New total for each pirate	141	94	47	282
	(50%)	(33 ⅓%)	(16 ⅔%)	

COUNTER *page 94*
Two-thirds

HORSE RACING *page 95*

No	Cecil	Bertie	Clarence	Percival	Cuthbert	Claude
1	✓			✓	✓	
2		✓	✓	✓		
3	✓	✓		✓		
4			✓	✓	✓	
5	✓	✓		✓		
6			✓	✓		
7	✓	✓		✓		
8			✓	✓		
9	✓			✓	✓	
10			✓			✓
11	✓	✓				
12			✓			
13	✓	✓				

Only one tick will indicate a true answer so number 12 won.

CREATURES *page 96*
In order:
eel yak asp boa wren bull cow hart hind ape seal
ant vole collie fox bat

SQUARES AND TRIANGLES *page 96*

DAUGHTERS *page 97*
24 20 16 12

FARMERS *page 98*
Farmer Turnip 49   Farmer Wheat 35

SERIES *page 98*
AU First two letters of months of the year

RATS *page 99*
14 rats

TRAVELLERS *page 99*
24 miles   Half past three

FOOTMEN *page 100*
No engine driver lives on barley sugar.

TRAINS *page 101*
19

CASINO *page 102*

	A	B	C	D	E	F		A	B	C	D	E	F
1		✓		✓		✓	19	✓	✓				
2	✓		✓		✓	✓	20	✓				✓	
3		✓	✓			✓	21	✓				✓	
4	✓			✓		✓	22	✓				✓	
5		✓	✓			✓	23	✓	✓	✓		✓	
6	✓					✓	24	✓				✓	
7		✓	✓			✓	25	✓			✓	✓	
8	✓					✓	26	✓				✓	
9		✓		✓		✓	27	✓				✓	
10	✓						28	✓				✓	
11		✓	✓				29	✓	✓			✓	
12	✓			✓			30	✓					
13		✓	✓				31	✓	✓				
14	✓						32	✓				✓	
15		✓					33	✓					
16	✓			✓			34	✓					
17		✓	✓				35	✓					
18	✓						36	✓			✓		

Answer: 2. As two of them had lied, four had told the truth. Each tick indicates a true answer.

Therefore only the number 2 showing 4 ticks can be the correct choice.

SACKS *page 103*
1. 5.5 lbs 2. 6.5 lbs 3. 7 lbs 4. 4.5 lbs 5. 3.5 lbs

STATION *page 104*
8d
Solve by Algebra:
Let L = lemonade
   S = sandwich
   B = biscuit
   Then (a) 1L + 3S + 7B = 14
       (b) 1L + 4S + 10B = 17
Subtract (a) from (b) = S + 3B = 3
          or S = 3 – 3B
Substitute value of S in (a)
         L – 2B = 5
         or L = 5 + 2B
Now, for the cost of one of each, substitute:
        L + S + B = (5 + 2B) + (3 – 3B) + B = 8

GARDEN *page 105*
$\dfrac{30 \times 30 - 1}{2} = 449$ feet

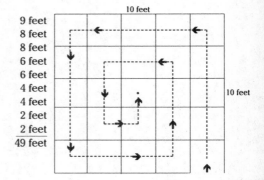

9 feet
8 feet
8 feet
6 feet
6 feet
4 feet
4 feet
2 feet
2 feet
——
49 feet

DOUBLET V *page 106*

R	I	V	E	R
R	O	V	E	R
C	O	V	E	R
C	O	V	E	S
C	O	R	E	S
C	O	R	N	S
C	O	I	N	S
C	H	I	N	S
S	H	I	N	S
S	H	I	N	E
S	H	O	N	E
S	H	O	R	E

FLUTES *page 107*
21
Every one else took 2. No 1 got only 1.
Example
$\dfrac{21}{11} = 1\dfrac{10}{11} + \dfrac{1}{11} = 2$ etc.

HEXAGRAM *page 108*
beaver   marmot   ferret   jaguar   heifer   donkey   *key*   badger

FARMERS *page 109*
Now the sheep had cost 10 guineas each and they had an odd number, so the first two digits of the total number of guineas received must be an odd number such as 19. We can then eliminate all even numbers such as 12. You will see that the third digit is always 6. This must be the value of the goat. Therefore the value of the 4 chickens must be 2 guineas.

Example: 256 guineas received (16 cows)
$$16 \times 16 = 256$$

	Thistle	Corncob
Sheep purchased	13 = 130	12 = 120
Goat purchased	– = –	1 = 6
	130	126
4 chickens	– 2	+ 2
	128	128 Answer 2 guineas

RIDDLE *page 110*
And dreaming of ten, dear,

PRISONER *page 111*

	A	B	C	D	E	F			A	B	C	D	E	F
1	✓			✓				11	✓		✓	✓		✓
2		✓						12	✓	✓	✓	✓	✓	
3	✓			✓				13	✓		✓	✓		✓
4		✓						14	✓	✓	✓			
5	✓							15	✓		✓	✓	✓	
6		✓		✓	✓			16	✓	✓	✓			
7	✓				✓			17	✓		✓	✓		
8		✓			✓			18	✓	✓	✓	✓		
9	✓			✓	✓			19	✓		✓	✓		
10		✓	✓	✓		✓		20			✓	✓		

As one had lied five had told the truth. Only 12 has 5 ✓ so 12 is the answer.

COMMON *page 112*
They each have 3 letters in alphabetical order.
Example: CANOPY

TRIANGLE *page 113*

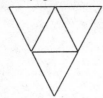

DOUBLE PALINDROMES *page 114*
Able was I ere I saw Elba.
Was it a car or a cat I saw?

STUCK UP *page 115*
Hoity Toity

ABRACADABRA *page 116*
$2^{10} = 1024$

GROUPS *page 117*

BUILDING	OF	ROOKS
COWARDICE	OF	CURS
HERD	OF	SWANS
SORD	OF	MALLARD
PRIDE	OF	LIONS
OBSERVANCE	OF	HERMITS
BLUSH	OF	BOYS
DESERT	OF	LAPWING
CONVOCATION	OF	EAGLES
COVERT	OF	COOTS

MAGIC SQUARE *page 118*

A	S	S	I	S	T
S	H	I	N	E	R
S	I	N	G	L	Y
I	N	G	L	E	S
S	E	L	E	C	T
T	R	Y	S	T	S

PAIRS *page 119*

BARREL	CHESTED	VILLAGE	GREEN
BEAUFORT	SCALE	UGLY	DUCKLING
ALMOND	BLOSSOM	TABLE	MANNERS
YELLOW	STREAK	SLEEPY	HOLLOW
WINTER	CHERRY	RABBIT	WARREN

Odd word STAMP

BITS AND PIECES *page 120*
anxious, acknowledge, bookkeeper, orphan-hood, Gesellschaft, pachyderm or brachydactyl, mezzo-relievo

MAGIC SQUARE *page 121*

D	R	A	M	A	S
R	E	T	I	R	E
A	T	O	M	I	C
M	I	M	O	S	A
A	R	I	S	E	N
S	E	C	A	N	T

WORDS *page 122*
All can be diminished by one letter (from beginning and end alternately) forming a new word each time.

LETTERS *page 122*
BIG-FACED

PAIRING *page 123*

	Solution 1		Solution 2
	WATER	TAP	ROOT
	ROOT	BEET	SUGAR
	SUGAR	DOUGHNUT	TORUS
	TORUS	RING	GOLD
	GOLD	MOIDORE	COIN
	COIN	PENNY	BLACK
	BLACK	WHITE	PALE
	PALE	FENCE	EPEE
	EPEE	SWORD	FISH
	FISH	SEA	WATER

VICTORIAN WORD SEARCH *page 124*

1. bedstaff   2. baselard   3. badelyng   4. fuzzock   5. drowsen
6. gozzard   7. doppy   8. deese   9. adeps   10. zax
11. rea   12. lat   13. eik   14. taj   15. zho   16. ea

KNIGHT'S MOVE *page 125*

Beware of the employee heralded as a man ahead of his time; on Wednesday he'll be wishing it were Friday.

TRICKY *page 126*

'just one word'

CHARLOTTE *page 126*

4 years ago

ARAB *page 127*

Asterisk – 'Ass to risk'

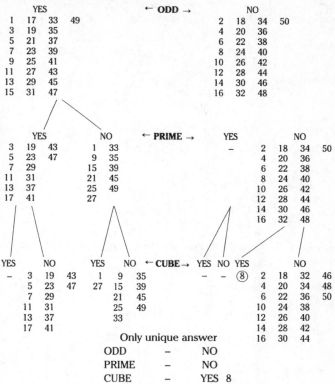

	YES			← ODD →		NO		
1	17	33	49		2	18	34	50
3	19	35			4	20	36	
5	21	37			6	22	38	
7	23	39			8	24	40	
9	25	41			10	26	42	
11	27	43			12	28	44	
13	29	45			14	30	46	
15	31	47			16	32	48	

	YES			NO		← PRIME →	YES		NO			
3	19	43	1	33			–	2	18	34	50
5	23	47	9	35				4	20	36	
7	29		15	39				6	22	38	
11	31		21	45				8	24	40	
13	37		25	49				10	26	42	
17	41		27					12	28	44	
								14	30	46	
								16	32	48	

YES	NO			YES	NO	← CUBE →	YES NO YES		NO		
–	3	19	43	1	9	35	– – ⑧	2	18	32	46
	5	23	47	27	15	39		4	20	34	48
	7	29			21	45		6	22	36	50
	11	31			25	49		10	24	38	
	13	37			33			12	26	40	
	17	41						14	28	42	
								16	30	44	

Only unique answer

ODD	–	NO
PRIME	–	NO
CUBE	–	YES 8

BARREL *page 128*

Tip up the barrel
until the rum is
level with the top.

If you **cannot** see any
part of the bottom of
the barrel it is more
than half full.

If you **can** see part
of the bottom of the
barrel then it is less
than half full.

ANAGRAMS *page 129*
1. racoon   2. leopard   3. terrier   4. lioness   5. samoyed
6. spaniel   7. carthorse   8. african lion

MONTH *page 130*

	A	B	C	D	E	F
January	✓			✓	✓	✓
February					✓	✓
March		✓		✓		
April		✓	✓			
May				✓		✓
June	✓		✓			
July	✓			✓		✓
August				✓	✓	
September		✓		✓		
October				✓	✓	
November		✓		✓		
December				✓	✓	

Only a month with 3 ✓ indicates three true answers, so July is the answer.

OCTAHEDRAL DICE *page 131*
Not fair

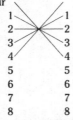

There are 64 possible combinations (8 × 8), and 5 ways of throwing 6 (see above); therefore there are 5 chances in 64.

Probability p = 0·78125; the casino *could* pay 12 to 1.

CHILDREN *page 131*
2 – 5 – 8 – 11 – 14 – 17 – 20 – 23 – 26

Thus, 2 (4) + 5 (25) + 8 (64) + 11 (121)
+ 14 (196) + 17 (289) + 20 (400)
+ 23 (529) + 26 (676) = 48 (2304).

MURDERER IN THE MANSION *page 132*
Allen

THE VILLAGE HALL *page 133*
10

Divide by 3. All the ladies had three items.
The remainder shows the number of ladies who had 4.

85
75
60
90
———
$310 \div 3 = 100 + \underline{10}$ remainder

POEMS *page 134*
All of your poems are uninteresting.

SPIDER'S WEB *page 135*

Step 1	20 inches	
	x 4	
	80 inches	= Circumference
Step 2	80	
	3.14	= 25.48 Diameter
Step 3	25.48^2	= 649.23 Area of square
Step 4	25.48	
	2	= 12.74 Radius of circle
Step 5	12.74^2	
	x 3.14	
	509.65	= Area of circle
Step 6	649.23	
	− 509.65	
	139.58	= Area of corners
Step 7	139.58	
	4	= 34.9 Square Inches (Area of web)